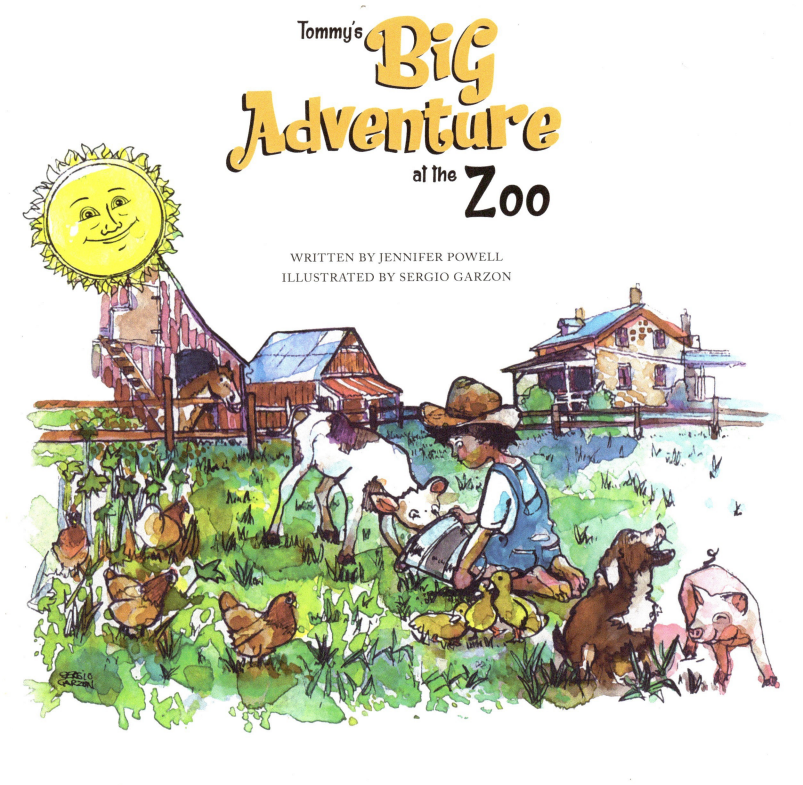

Tommy's Big Adventure at the Zoo

WRITTEN BY JENNIFER POWELL
ILLUSTRATED BY SERGIO GARZON

TEXT COPYRIGHT © 2017 JENNIFER POWELL
ILLUSTRATION COPYRIGHT © 2017 JENNIFER POWELL
ALL RIGHTS RESERVED

ISBN-13: 978-0692990094
ISBN-10: 0692990097

Dedicated with love to my sweet family.

Early one morning,
the sun's brilliant rays,
peeked through Tommy's window,
looking to play.

It searched through his covers,
and over the farm,
and finally found him
outside near the barn.

"Where are you going?"

the sun seemed to say.

"Where are you off to so early today?"

"I'm moving my family
of ducks to the zoo!
There's a beautiful pond,
and shady trees too."

"The zookeeper invited them
over to stay.
You can come along too;
keep us warm on the way."

Tom quickly got ready,
packed food for his ducks,
then gently he set them
in all his toy trucks.

He tied them together,
his ducks tucked in safe;
a train full of ducklings
and trucks on their way.

Once through the gates

he looked to his left...

then looked to his right.

Where was the pond?

It was nowhere in sight!

What lay before him

was a colorful maze.

This would be harder

than he planned on today.

The first path he took
he found zebras at play;
jumping and splashing
around in the shade.

This path had amazing
giant-sized trees;
trunks that were massive;
a cool canopy.

Somewhere in the zoo
was the pond for his ducks;
perhaps the next tree
would bring him good luck.

But this tree was already
home to the monkeys!
Swinging like acrobats;
flipping with ease.

He laughed as we watched them,
all playful and free,
and his ducks waddled close
to the young chimpanzees.

Tom walked down the hill
'till he saw something new!
A fluffed, feathery bird,
called an emu.

"What a strange looking bird,"
thought Tom as he passed.
And then a sound caught his ear;
had he found it at last?

Tom could hear water...
...from right over there!
A stream? To the pond?
Could he finally be there?

No!
It was home
to the hippos,
all playful
and wet!

Tom tugged
on his trucks;
he wasn't
there yet.

So onward he walked,
uphill and down;
meeting lions
and rhinos,
the world
all around.

Giraffes and flamigos,
elephants, seals;
Polar bears, caribou,
gators, and eels.

Tom walked the whole zoo, each animal town.

His feet were quite sore; his heart in a frown.

"My feet are so sore,

and I'm tired and hot.

Maybe we *never*

will find the right spot!"

As he sat there, poor Tommy, too tired to go;

the sun called down and encouraged him so:

"Keep looking! You'll make it!

You'll find it -- I know!"

Tom's feet were so tired; his legs achingly sore.

But looking ahead...

...there was just one place more.

He came to the biggest hill yet he had faced.

To the top he pulled slowly,

but steadily paced.

Just when he felt

the last steps he could take,

with the sun at his back,

his strength almost to break.

He crested the hill and collapsed at the top;

he had given his all, to the very last drop.

"You're amazing my boy! the sun whispered so sweet.

"Open your eyes, you have someone to meet."

Blinking upward he looked,

and he noticed a man;

tall, slender, and beaming,

and lending a hand.

"You've done it my boy!

I'm so glad you've come!

You traveled the path

and the quest you have won!"

"You're stronger than ever. You're brillant and tall.

You've made it my boy!

You've conquered it all!"

Then lifting sweet Tommy to stand near his side,

he showed him the view and smiled with pride.

For just down the hill,

in the warm setting sun...

...there was the pond;

the most beautiful one.

CPSIA information can be obtained
at www.ICGtesting.com
Printed in the USA
BVHW02*0157060118
504558BV00007B/49/P

9 780692 995389